WOLVES
Among Sheep

Beware of False Ministers With Mermaid Powers

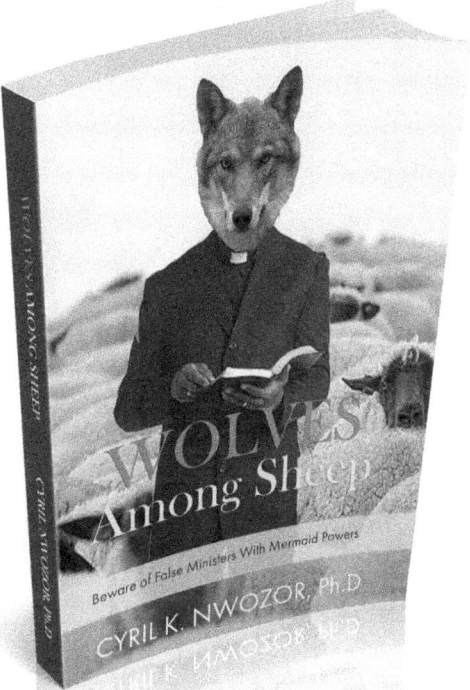

WOLVES
Among Sheep

Beware of False Ministers With Mermaid Powers

CYRIL K. NWOZOR, Ph.D

REHOBOTH HOUSETM

WOLVES AMONG SHEEP

Copyright © 2018 By Cyril K. Nwozor, Ph.D

ISBN:978-1-64301-014-4

This book is published in the United States of America by Rehoboth House, Chicago and protected under the United States Copyright Laws.

The opinions expressed by the author in this book are exclusively his and not those of Rehoboth House.

Unless otherwise indicated, all scripture quotations are taken from the Authorized King James Version of the Holy Bible (KJV).

Forward enquiries to Cyril K. Nwozor for teachings, seminars, and workshops:

Email: kandyril@yahoo.com or call +1871-298-1862

Placing Online Order for the Book Visit
Amazon.com, barnesandnoble.com, and other Online Bookstores.
Author's website: cyrilnwozor.com

Interior and Cover Designed by Rehoboth House, Chicago
www.rehobothhouseonline.com
email:info@rehobothhouseonline.com

REHOBOTH HOUSE

TABLE OF CONTENTS

Dedication

I dedicate this book to the Church of Jesus Christ and her leadership, whom He purchased with His own blood on the Cross of Calvary.

"So guard yourselves and God's people. Feed and shepherd God's flock—his church, purchased with his own blood—over which the Holy Spirit has appointed you as leaders" (Acts 20:28 NLT).

Reflection

Personal Notes:_____

_____

_____

_____

_____

_____

_____

_____

_____

Guided Action Plan

_____

_____

_____

_____

_____

_____

_____

Acknowledgment

I first of all humbly acknowledge God, our Father for who He is. Father, from age to age there is none like you! For in you we live, and move, and have our being. You have been our help from ages past that we can confidently say; *Though an army may encamp against us, our hearts shall not fear; Though war should rise against us, In this we will be confident. Psalm 27:3 (Paraphrased).*

Thank you, Father, we love You always.

I sincerely acknowledge my beloved wife and friend; Deborah Ifey for her unflinching support and encouragement. My love, I say thank you for standing faithfully and letting God do what He knows how to do best. You are again my forerunner, my best friend and my love. Remember, there is nothing impossible for God. With Him, all things are possible. I want to assure you that *"The LORD is your shepherd, and His goodness and mercy shall follow you all the days of your life."*

God richly bless you. I love you dearly.

Also, I acknowledge our son Cyril Kanayor Nwozor, Jr. I see God in His perfect promises guiding your footsteps as you progress further in life. Now you are older and graduated from Bowie High School. As you embark on your undergraduate studies, I want to say thank you for your dedication and excellent work. We give God all the glory for your life.

We love you dearly.

Prelude

False Pastors With Mermaid Anointing

"And Jesus answered and said unto them, Take heed that no man deceive you. For many shall come in my name, saying, I am Christ; and shall deceive many. And ye shall hear of wars and rumours of wars: see that ye be not troubled: for all these things must come to pass, but the end is not yet. For nation shall rise against nation, and kingdom against kingdom: and there shall be famines, and pestilences, and earthquakes, in divers' places. All these are the beginning of sorrows. Then shall they deliver you up to be afflicted, and shall kill you: and ye shall be hated of all nations for my name's sake. And then shall many be offended, and shall betray one another, and shall hate one another. And many false prophets shall rise, and shall deceive many. And because iniquity shall abound, the love of many shall wax cold. But he that shall endure unto the end, the same shall be saved" (Matt. 24:4-13).

As the Day of the Lord approaches, the battle of the souls of men is intensified. Satan has deployed his envoys all over the world to deceive and darken the hearts of men, and ultimately destroy as many souls he can. These satanic emissaries consist of pretenders that camouflage as ministers of light. Every category of false servants of God belongs to this cohort of darkness.

> *"These people are false apostles. They are deceitful workers who disguise themselves as apostles of Christ. But I am not surprised! Even Satan disguises himself as an angel of light" (2Corinthians 11:13 NLT).*

Satan has anointed them with his spirit of deception and equip these self-made pastors and ministers of the gospel with the spirit of manipulation. Their mandate is to lure people away from the Lord and the path of eternity to committing apostasy; giving heed to seducing spirits, and to the doctrines of devils, etc. They corrupt the simplicity of the gospel and denying the Lord who bought them with His blood, because of their greed and proclivity for material acquisition.

The true confession of the young pastor in chapter one is an evidence of the pervasiveness of this deception in the Church. As you read this book, What I say to you, I say to all "WATCH!

> *"Now the Spirit speaketh expressly, that in the latter times some shall depart from the faith, giving heed to seducing spirits, and doctrines of devils; speaking lies in hypocrisy; having their conscience seared with a hot iron" (1Tim. 4:1-2).*

Introduction

Ever since the creation of man, God has always use prophets. Since the days of Adam and Eve to Noah, Abraham, Moses, Elijah, and Elisha, etc., there have been prophets on the earth at different dispensation. A prophet is a man called by God to be His spokesman on earth. When a prophet speaks, God indirectly is speaking. The experiences of these great men of God in those days provoked and inspired people at the time.

Abraham was a prophet, and God severally spoke to him and made promises about his future and his posterity. Moses was an Old Testament prophet used by God to lead thousands of His people out of the bondage and slavery of Egypt. He was considered a humble Prophet than any other man. The Bible says:

"And here arose not a prophet since in Israel like unto Moses, whom the LORD knew face to face," (Deut. 34:10).

Elijah was a prophet and a miracle worker who appeared with Moses at the transfiguration of our Lord. He was a man who has no antecedent as a prophet and suddenly emerged on the scene but has been standing before the Lord. His exit from this life was even more dramatic.

If God chooses a person as a prophet or prophetess, the person must receive directions and revelations from Him. Unfortunately, we are witnessing a different scenario in our generation. We know that God communicates to the Church through His servants, but these last days, many false Apostles, Prophets, Evangelist, Pastors, and Teachers of the gospel are all over the world. It is increasingly becoming difficult to distinguish between the true servants of God and the false. These company of men and women claim that they heard from God when God did not speak to them. Their lifestyle and ministry are at variance and inconsistent with the gospel. Their focus in ministry is on miracles and material acquisition.

"For I have told you often before, and I say it again with tears in my eyes, that there are many whose conduct shows they are really enemies of the cross of Christ. They are headed for destruction. Their god is their appetite, they brag about shameful things, and they think only about this life here on earth. But we are citizens of heaven, where the

Lord Jesus Christ lives. And we are eagerly waiting for him to return as our Savior" (Philippians 3:18-20 NLT).

"And he said, Hear now my words: If there be a prophet among you, I the LORD will make myself known unto him in a vision, and will speak unto him in a dream" (Num. 12:6).

"After these things the word of the LORD came to Abram in a vision, saying, "Do not be afraid, Abram. I am your shield, your exceedingly great reward" (Gen. 15:1).

Reflection

Personal Notes:_____

_____

_____

_____

_____

_____

_____

_____

_____

Guided Action Plan

_____

_____

_____

_____

_____

_____

Chapter One

A True Life Confession Of A Pastor

This was a true confession made by a pastor of a particular church in Kaduna State, Nigeria. Due to certain reasons, the names of the persons involved were deleted or blanked out. The scriptures in between this confession are inserted by the author.

"Why You Should Be Very Careful What Church you attend and "so-called" Men of God You Follow."

The Pastor's Confession Begins

"My name is ...., I am a pastor, but I have disappointed God, and I really don't know where to begin to tell my story. I must tell you the truth. I can't really say if I have a call or not. I was a Sunday school teacher in my church for nine years at Kaduna, Nigeria. In 1999 I was led to start a church, but from the experiences I have gathered now, I cannot say certainly that I was led by the Holy Spirit to start that church.

As of 2008, I was not making any progress both spiritually and materially. I saw many churches which began several years after mine, and they were making waves and are still making progress. At a point, I did not know what to do again, and after discussing with my wife, I decided to approach the General Overseer of a church that began seven years after I started my ministry. I explained to him that personally, I was not making any headway and same with my ministry. My ministry would grow up to 200 people, and after a short period it would shrink to 50 people, and at times it would grow to 150 and shrink to 40 people. I approached him because the growth in his church was fast and consistent. He began the church in 2006, and by 2012 he was recording 11,000 people on a Sunday service, and he was also making good money and riding in big cars, including the latest jeeps.

After listening to me, he promised to help me solve my problem. He said I needed to be empowered and that it is going to cost me some amount of money; and that I need to have a big and strong heart. Then he asked me if I have got a strong heart? And I told him that I have, as long as it is not going to involve killing a fellow human being. He asked me thrice if I have got a strong heart and I consistently gave him the same answer. Again he asked me if I want single empowerment or double empowerment, and I asked him which one was better, and he said double empowerment was better, but it would cost me a lot of money, and that after the empowerment I was going to be told how to maintain and renew the power.

The Bible Says:

> "But know this, that in the last days perilous times will come." (2Ti 3:1)

> "For there shall arise false Christs, and false prophets, and shall shew great signs and wonders; insomuch that, if it were possible, they shall deceive the very elect." (Matt 24:24)

> "Let no man deceive you by any means: for that day shall not come, except there come a falling away first, and that man of sin be revealed, the son of perdition." (2 Thess. 2:3)

The Confession Continues

This time I became afraid, and I asked him if the maintenance and renewal involved any ritual, he said no, that whatever the renewal and maintenance will involve are just normal things that I was already doing so I should not be afraid. He said I should go and raise three hundred and fifty thousand Naira (350,000), equivalent to One thousand dollars ($1000.00) which I had to borrow from my wife. The next day I handed over the money to him, and he asked me to go and get ready that we shall be going to Lagos and Port-Harcourt. (Nigeria). I got ready, and we took flight from Abuja to Lagos that same day.

In Lagos, we lodged at the guest house of a big ministry, and at 11.30 p.m. we went out in a private car to the Bar-Beach. At the Bar-Beach we were at the bank when he spoke some unknown language and told me that a woman was going to come out of the water and that I should do whatever she says. As soon as he said that, there was rumbling on the surface of the water, and a mermaid came out of it. The general overseer told me not to be afraid that the mermaid will not harm me, so I picked courage when I saw her.

When she came to the surface of the water, the lower part of her body was like that of a fish. My eyes were transfixed to that lower part, and as she was getting closer to me, it became human. Then she came to me and asked me to have sex with her which I did in the presence of the general overseer. After having sex with her, she put her hand in her vagina and made a sign of the cross on my forehead and my palm and told me that she had empowered me and that I would see the difference.

The Scripture Says:

"And deceiveth them that dwell on the earth by the means of those miracles which he had power to do in the sight of the beast; saying to them that dwell on the earth, that they should make an image to the beast, which had the wound by a sword, and did live" (Revelation 13:14).

The mermaid left me, went to the General Overseer and brought out a golden cross and chain from her stomach and wore it on the neck of the general overseer who gave her some money. The mermaid thanked him and went back into the sea. All the time she spoke in English language.

When we eventually got back to the ministry's guest house, the general overseer told me that we have to go to the church of that ministry because they were having a night vigil. When we got there I was given an opportunity to minister in the church, and as I raised my hands from the altar the members began to fall on themselves, and some were tumbling on others. I must say, I was almost embarrassed because I never expected the manifestation of the mermaid power to be so soon. After the all-night service, we went back to the guest house, and the general overseer asked me if I was happy the way the power manifested, and I said yes. He told me that we should go to bed and get some sleep because we would be going to Port-Harcourt that evening.

That afternoon before we went to Port-Harcourt, as I was sleeping, that same mermaid I had sex with at the Bar-beach came to me in my dream and told me that to maintain and also constantly renew the power I must be having sex with a virgin once every month, so this jolted me out of sleep. I went to the general overseer's room to explain what I saw and heard in my dream, and he said it was no problem. When I asked him how I was going to be getting the virgins, he said he was going to assist me to get them, but I needed to pay for his service. Honestly Apostle after this I wanted to back out, but I had no courage to say or do so.

TAKE NOTE: While at the Bar-Beach, Lagos, Nigeria, I saw many pastors who came there with other senior pastors. It was like a tradition. There must be a senior pastor bringing in younger pastors, and I believe each senior pastor had a particular mermaid they relate with because I saw up to ten mermaids attending to some other young pastors.

The Scripture Says:

"But evil men and impostors will grow worse and worse, deceiving and being deceived. But you must continue in the things which you have learned and been assured of, knowing from whom you have learned them, and that from

*childhood you have known the Holy Scriptures, which are
able to make you wise for salvation through faith which is
in Christ Jesus" (2Ti 3:13-15).*

The Confession Continues

In the evening we were at the local airport in Lagos, and
we took a flight to Port-Harcourt. At Port-Harcourt,
we lodged in the guest house of another ministry, and
at midnight we got out, eventually arriving in a very big
compound of a woman called Eze-Nwanyi (chief of the
goddess). Inside the compound were many houses.

We met many pastors there including first generation
church pastors. When it was my turn, the general overseer
paid some money and itemized what should be done for
me. When I went into the room, I was surprised it was
a woman again and as I was thinking – woman again! I
found myself on top of the woman on a bed in an adjacent
room. Honestly, I have not been able to recall how I found
myself on that bed. I had sex with her and also sucked
her breasts. After the sexual session, she made some sound
like "animal cry" and administered some stuff into my eyes,
and I began immediately to see into the spirit world and
also discussed with some spirit beings. After that, she gave
me a bottle of olive oil which she called "do as I say." She
said when I use this olive oil, the members of my church
will do whatever I ask them to do.

She also gave me another bottle of olive oil which she called "all seeing oil." She said with the oil I could see deep into people's secrets, and a bottle of olive oil which she called "slaying oil" for slaying people (under "so-called" anointing) during prayer. She finally gave me two more bottles of olive oil. The first one is "crowd pulling oil" and the second one is "touch and follow" – which I will be using to hypnotize women especially virgins because I will be having sex with them and married women to renew the empowerment. She said I could have sex and immediately after that I could go straight into ministration without having my bath. She bound me with an oath of secrecy.

We left that same midnight and went back to the lodge, and the general overseer told me to rub the "touch and follow" oil; then we went to the vigil of the church in which we were lodging in their guest house. I was allowed to minister, and I busted into prophecy to my own astonishment. In the morning two virgins were sent to the general overseer, and he gave me one. So we took them to the guest house and had sex with them. What really surprised me was that the young girls never asked where we were taking them to and why we were taking them there, which is unusual for virgin girls.

When the girls left, the general overseer told me that from then onwards I had to concentrate my sermons around prosperity and stop preaching salvation and righteousness messages. He said I should be sending tithes to him and that he knew how part of the tithes would get to the woman at Port-Harcourt. Eventually, we left Port-Harcourt to Abuja and back to Kaduna. When I began service after my return, things began to change. Money began to come, the crowd also began to come, and within one week miracles, deliverance followed; prosperity began to happen in the church, the spirit of prophecy came in like I had never seen it in my life."

Here Is What The Scripture Says:

"But there were false prophets also among the people, even as there shall be false teachers among you, who privily shall bring in damnable heresies, even denying the Lord that bought them and bring upon themselves swift destruction. And many shall follow their pernicious ways; because of whom, the way of truth shall be evil spoken of. And through covetousness shall they with feigned words make merchandise of you: whose judgment now of a long time lingereth not, and their damnation slumbereth not" (2Peter 2:1-3).

"For the time will come when they will not endure sound doctrine; but after their own lusts shall they heap to themselves teachers, having itching ears; And they shall turn away their ears from the truth, and shall be turned unto fables" (2Timothy 4:3-4).

Days Of Doom

"Be not deceived; God is not mocked: for whatsoever a man soweth, that shall he also reap. For he that soweth to his flesh shall of the flesh reap corruption; but he that soweth to the Spirit shall of the Spirit reap life everlasting" (Gal 6:7-8).

The Confession Continues

I have been having sex with virgin girls, and married women and things have been working out fine for my family and the church for the past six years, but I have gotten to a stage in which I am no longer feeling comfortable with the whole thing. I have had dreams in which I saw myself burning in hell. I have had this dream of hell seven times, and in one of the dreams, I awoke only for the same dream to continue when I went back to bed. I have had sleepless nights, and many nights I get raped by that same mermaid. I have lost two of my children mysteriously but through the same pattern. For the past three months, I have not been able to get virgin girls, and this has affected the power as it is going down.

I want to get out of this whole issue even if it means closing the church. I have gone to the general overseer, and he said it was too late for me to get out. He threatened me with a mysterious death. He said it is not possible for me to turn against the mermaid and Eze-Nwanyi (chief of the goddess) because they were already part of my life. I told him that I will do everything positively possible to get myself out of this. Three days later two men approached me and told me that if I love my life, I should vanish from Kaduna because they have been paid by the general overseer to eliminate me, so I had to close the church and left the town finally after two days."

'For, lo, they that are far from thee shall perish: thou hast destroyed all them that go a whoring from thee" (Psalm 73:27).

THE PASTOR SOUGHT FOR HELP

The Confession Continues

As I am writing to you now, I have nothing to hold on to but only God Almighty. The problem is that God seems to be very far from me no matter how much and fervently I have been calling on Him and asking for His mercies. I know I have offended Him, but I know He is a God of a second chance. I have read your books – Overcoming the Queen of the Coast series, and I strongly believe you are the only one that God can use to help me out of this physical hell I have put myself. I am really afraid of going to meet any other person (man of God) because those who are using devilish powers are more than those who use the power of God.

For some time now I have not been sleeping at night and me also at times hallucinate. Sir, I urgently need your help because I believe the time is running out for me as the attack from the marine kingdom increases. No other pastor has exposed them like you. I know I have transferred many spirits into so many people and I want to know what I can do so that those people can be free from these wicked and evil spirits.

Apostle, it is really unfortunate that the Church of our Lord Jesus Christ has been taken over by Mermaids. The number of pastors using marine spirits is alarming, and more of them are getting initiated daily into this wicked kingdom. So these pastors are also initiating their spiritually illiterate members. Before I messed up myself spiritually, I had always wondered why members of churches follow their pastors sheepishly, but now I know better.

The marine kingdom is working day and night to overtake the Church, and unfortunately, the Church is sleeping. In the last two months, I have had four car crashes, and I know they want to eliminate me, but God has been my helper and my only hope. They have killed my two children, and now they want me dead. I am becoming afraid of staying alone because of some bizarre spiritual appearances I see, and things have started to move in my brain and body. Any time I start praying the movement would start, and sometimes I feel the movement in my marrow.

The greatest need I have now is to be forgiven by God. If I can get His forgiveness, I don't mind dying after that because I really don't want to go to hell. I have been misled by the General Overseer just as so many young pastors have been misled by their General Overseers and Senior Pastors. Sir, I know you are a very busy person. I will appreciate if you find time to pray over this my problems and seek the face of the Lord on how He will use you to help me out. I know that if I am forgiven, my deliverance will be easy. I regret selling my soul to marine spirits. The Eze-Nwanyi (goddess) is also a very strong agent of the mermaid.

I look forward to hearing from you; your co-servant in the Lord, Pastor "........................"

The Helping Pastor's Response

When I received this letter, I called the number over three times, but it was switched off. So the next day I called, and it went through. A woman took the call and when I asked to speak to Pastor "............." I was told that he had died in a car crash the previous day. I was dumbfounded. I just expressed my condolences to the woman who later told me that she was his wife that she had to amend her ways with the Lord and move ahead with her life. She expressed gratitude and thanked me.

After I cut off the discussion, I was frozen to a spot for over five minutes until my son came and touched me asking what the matter was. I must say that it is very unfortunate this pastor died. Those of us alive need to be extremely careful about what we do and where we place our hands. When we want success by worldly standards, we can easily soil our hands. I know that if he had not started to get out of these evil powers, they wouldn't have killed him. Only God knows if he was forgiven before his sudden death. If not, no one needs to tell you his destination by now. We must make choices in life and whatever choices we make there are consequences, and we should be ready to accept the consequences of the choices we have made. God is not going to hold the general overseer responsible for the sin of the young pastor. May God help us to be watchful, wise, and to wait for Him to fight on our behalf instead of seeking and succumbing to worldly and devilish means for help!"

"I call heaven and earth to record this day against you, that I have set before you, life and death, blessing and cursing: therefore choose life, that both thou and thy seed. That thou mayest love the LORD thy God, and that thou mayest obey his voice, and that thou mayest cleave unto him: for he is thy life, and the length of thy days: that thou mayest dwell in the land which the LORD sware unto thy fathers, to Abraham, to Isaac, and to Jacob, to give them" (Deut. 30:19-20).

"And he said unto them, He that hath ears to hear, let him hear" (Mark 4:9).

Reflection

Personal Notes:
_____

_____

_____

_____

_____

_____

_____

_____

_____

Guided Action Plan

_____

_____

_____

_____

_____

_____

Chapter Two

Wake Up From Slumber

"And we know that we are of God, and the whole world lieth in wickedness" (1 John 5:19).

The mystery of iniquity is becoming so prevalent in our days that everyone needs to wake up from slumber and guard our loins with truth. Believe it or not, *the whole world is under* the sway of the *evil one* as we witness the rise of false pastors and ministers around the world. Satan knows that his time is short, therefore in his desperation, he is deploying many false men and women of God all over the world and equipping them to deceive, destroy, kill, and steal. His ultimate goal is to finally take as many as he could to eternal damnation in hell.

Paul Said:

> *"For I know this that after my departure savage wolves will come in among you not sparing the flock. "Also from among yourselves, men will rise up, speaking perverse things, to draw away the disciples after themselves"* (Acts 20:29-30).

The most dangerous enemies which the Church has, have been nurtured in its own bosom, and have consisted of those who have perverted the true doctrines of the gospel. They proclaim doctrines tending to distract and deceive people. They are men under the influence of ambition; love of money, power, and popularity.

As children of God, it is our obligations to be watchmen, warning everyone to beware of these false pastors who lie in wait to ensnare and destroy the faithful.

> *"Be sober, be vigilant; because your adversary the devil walks about like a roaring lion, seeking whom he may devour"* (1Pe 5:8).

There are reasons why we should be sober and vigilant; we have an active, implacable, subtle enemy to contend with. He walks about the world recruiting false men and women of God. He uses them everywhere to have access to people, and oppose them in his best interests. Through these deceivers who are his agents, he gets to know your feelings and your propensities and informs himself of all the circumstances of your life.

The scripture says, the enemy is seeking whom he may devour. The implication is that he can't devour everyone. Those who are sober and vigilant are proof against him. He can never devour them. Those who are not watchful and are drunken with the cares of this world, are easy prey to him.

Awake and be alert. Always be watchful to what is happening around you. Never be off your guard and take things for granted. Your enemies are always alert waiting to pray against the gullible. They are never off their guards. Have a divine vision rising from the word of God to guide you. It is the infallible and unadulterated word of God that is your only defense and security. You can be assured of it in this perilous times we are living in.

> "But the end of all things is at hand; therefore be serious and watchful in your prayers" (1Pe 4:7).

> "And do this, understanding the present time. The hour has come for you to wake up from your slumber because our salvation is nearer now than when we first believed" (Romans 13:11).

When Apostle Paul was writing to the congregation of new Christians at the heart of the Roman Empire, he began by explaining to them of the doctrines they are to believe. He spoke to them about the kind of life Christian teaching must produce in their lives. He spoke and addressed both their individual lives and the life of the Church. He went on to reference the Law of God and then urged them to love their neighbors as themselves.

At this point, you would think that he has covered all the spectrum of Christian living, but he still has something else to say about discipleship. He turned to the theme of "Revived and Revitalized Christianity." He was concerned about some of them growing lukewarm. Some were leaving their first love for other interest such as business and politics; etc. In fact, many were backsliding without being aware of it. The picture Paul painted here was of a Christian drifting off to sleep.

> *"Ye are all the children of light, and the children of the day: we are not of the night, nor of darkness. Therefore let us not sleep, as do others; but let us watch and be sober"* *(1Thess.5-6).*

Fight The Good Fight Of Faith

Our honors, our lives and our souls are at stake. Therefore, we have to content earnestly for them. Live the life of the Gospel, and defend the cause of God. Expel the debauched, shamelessly immoral, unmask hypocrites, purge and build up the Church of Christ. Live in the Spirit of Christ, and give yourself wholly to this work and fight the good fight of faith.

> *"Fight the good fight of faith, lay hold on eternal life, whereunto thou art also called, and hast professed a good profession before many witnesses" (1 Timothy 6:12).*

> *" If anyone teaches otherwise and does not consent to wholesome words, even the words of our Lord Jesus Christ, and to the doctrine which accords with godliness, 4he is proud, knowing nothing, but is obsessed with disputes and arguments over words, from which come envy, strife, reviling, evil suspicions, useless wranglings of men of corrupt minds and destitute of the truth, who suppose that godliness is a means of gain. From such withdraw yourself" (1 Timothy 6:3-5).*

The allusion to the public games is still carried on all over the world. You have been called at such a time as this. You have been chosen as one proper to enter the lists of kingdom warriors in the presence of many witnesses. You have been called to take the necessary engagements against the false pastors and their doctrines. Many eyes are on you to see whether you will fight fearlessly and be faithful.

What good are the doctrines of Jesus Christ to the world if we are in slumber? What good is it that people believed that you have become moral and righteous if you are in slumber? What good is your church attendance when you are aware of the problems in God's kingdom and remain sleepy and docile?

In Scripture, believers are frequently exhorted to wake up and to be revived. They are warned of the dangers of spiritual slumber. Thus, it is time for you to be wise and wake up your slumbering spirit and resist what all these false pastors are doing in your lives, families, churches, communities, and nations. Proverbs advised:

> "Give no sleep to your eyes, nor slumber to your eyelids. Deliver yourself like a gazelle from the hand of the hunter, And like a bird from the hand of the fowler. Go to the ant, you sluggard! Consider her ways and be wise. How long will you slumber, O sluggard? When will you rise from your sleep?" (Proverbs 6:4-6, 9).

Resist Them

> "Submit yourselves therefore to God. Resist the devil, and he will flee from you. Draw near to God, and He will draw near to you. Cleanse your hands, you sinners; and purify your hearts, you double-minded" (James 4:7-8).

While you yield to God in all things, you are to yield to the devil in none. You are to resist and oppose him steadfastly in whatever way he may approach you, whether by allurements, fascinations of the world, flattering promises, temptation, or by threats. Satan makes his way, and secures his triumphs, rather by art, cunning, deception, and threatening than by true courage; and when opposed courageously, he flees.

If you are already into their snare, sort yourself out with God first, then find a sincere Bible preaching, Bible believing and Bible practicing Church and make every effort to remain free from the enemies captivity. The devil cannot conquer you if you continue to resist him in the Lord. Remember, he has been eternally defeated, destroyed and dethroned by the sacrificial death and triumphant resurrection of our Glorious King and Lord Jesus Christ. Never lose sight of the reality of the eternal victory of the Cross of Calvary. As defiant and stronger he may seem to be than any mortal man in the flesh, God would never permit him to conquer anyone who in Christ Jesus continues to resist him. He cannot force the human will. Whoever, in the name of JESUS, opposes the devil and his agents, is sure to have a speedy and glorious conquest.

"Finally, my brethren, be strong in the Lord and in the power of His might. Put on the whole armor of God that you may be able to stand against the wiles of the devil" (Eph. 6:10-11).

"Son of man, prophesy against the prophets of Israel that prophesy, and say thou unto them that prophesy out of their own hearts, Hear ye the word of the LORD; Thus saith the Lord GOD; Woe unto the foolish prophets, that follow their own spirit, and have seen nothing! They have seen vanity and lying divination, saying, The LORD saith: and the LORD hath not sent them: and they have made others to hope that they would confirm the word" (Ezekiel 13:2-3, 6).

Chapter Three

The False Pastors

Prophets were not only holy men of God among the Jews, who prophesied by divine inspiration, but there were also false prophets among them, whose prophecies were from their own imagination, and perverted the hearts of many from being allegiance to God. At a very early period of the Christian Church, many heresies sprung up. Heresies of destruction that if followed would lead a man to perdition. The Holy Spirit forewarned us through Apostle Peter. He foresaw these days of grand deception and the deluge of false ministers in the Church, parading themselves as messengers of God.

"But there were also false prophets among the people, even as there will be false teachers among you, who will secretly bring in destructive heresies, even denying the

Lord who bought them, and bring on themselves swift destruction" (2Pe 2:1).

When we speak of false prophets and pastors, we are talking of those who obviously advocate the false teaching of the true gospel of Jesus Christ and perverted the scriptures. They claim to have a large membership in the Body of Christ. They are those who without authority claim God's endorsement to their practices. They claim they have the gift of prophecy. Unfortunately, they are inspired by familiar spirits to manipulate and reap off their prey for their evil ends. False pastors and teachers are those who arrogantly attempt to imply new revelation and interpretations of the original word of God to deceive many.

They argue that the scriptures require new interpretations and they are qualified to offer such interpretations. They are self-appointed declarers of the gospel. They seek and attract followers with their false gospel by constantly sponsoring conferences, book publications, and journals. Jesus warned us of such people.

> *"And Jesus answered and said to them: "Take heed that no one deceives you. "For many will come in My name, saying, 'I am the Christ,' and will deceive many. "Then many false prophets will rise up and deceive many" (Mt 24:4-5, 11).*
>
> *"Beware of false prophets, who come to you in sheep's*

clothing, but inwardly they are ravenous wolves" (Mt 7:15).

Sheep is a symbol of obedience, humility, innocence, sincerity, and harmlessness. To come in sheep's clothing is to assume the appearance of sanctity, righteousness, and innocence when the heart is filled with evil tendencies. False pastors are teachers of wrong doctrines who come professing a commission from God, but their aims, however, are not to bring the heavenly treasure to the people, but to rob them of their earthly blessings. They are preachers for hire. Their motive for entering the ministry is to earn a living. They preach in many churches and plan conferences to get money to spend on their lusts. They confuse and manipulate people with feigned words, counterfeit tales, bogus miracles, and fascinating testimonies and stories that cannot be verified.

They are not interested in the truth, but only in leading as many people as possible astray, exploiting them with deceptive words. They have no divine credentials. They do not convert the heathen or the ungodly, for they have no divine unction. They are winds without cloud.

"These are wells without water, clouds that are carried with a tempest; to whom the mist of darkness is reserved forever. For when they speak great swelling words of vanity, they allure through the lusts of the flesh, through much wantonness, those that were clean escaped from them who live in error. While they promise them liberty,

they themselves are the servants of corruption: for of whom a man is overcome, of the same is he brought in bondage. For if after they have escaped the pollutions of the world through the knowledge of the Lord and Saviour Jesus Christ, they are again entangled therein, and overcome, the latter end is worse with them than the beginning" (2 Peter 2:17-20).

The church of God has been troubled by such pretend pastors; men who feed themselves and not the flocks; men who are too proud to humble themselves and too lazy to work. They have neither the grace nor the gifts to plant the standard of the cross on the Devil's territories.

"Now I beseech you, brethren, mark them which cause divisions and offences contrary to the doctrine which ye have learned; and avoid them. For they that are such serve not our Lord Jesus Christ, but their own belly; and by good words and fair speeches deceive the hearts of the simple" (Rom. 16:17-18).

Flattering Words

Flattery is one of the most powerful means these false pastors use to manipulate people who are simple-hearted. They use it to gain special attention. First, they come with smooth, plausible pretenses, as if they have a great love for truth. With an artful mingling of attention and flatteries on the minds of the unsuspecting, they draw people's hearts and affections towards themselves.

The Scripture Says:

> "For I know this that after my departure savage wolves will come in among you not sparing the flock. "Also from among yourselves, men will rise up, speaking perverse things, to draw away the disciples after themselves" (Ac 20:29-30).

These false teachers are crooked, perverted preventatives of God's kingdom and distracting doctrines; they mingle the true gospel with heathen practice. In other words, they practice syncretism None of them have been chosen, though they pretend to be inspired by the Spirit of God.

> "The coming of the lawless one is according to the working of Satan, with all power, signs, and lying wonders, and with all unrighteous deception among those who perish, because they did not receive the love of the truth, that they might be saved. And for this reason, God will send them strong delusion that they should believe the lie that they all may be condemned who did not believe the truth but had pleasure in unrighteousness" (2Thessalonian 2:9).

False pastors' work for Satan and, with every art of unrighteousness, and all the power which Satan can exhibit, they deceive many. They perform stage managed miracles to delude people. Those who run after them, the Bible says, God permits strong delusion to occupy their minds; so that they believe a lie rather than the truth.

"Beloved, believe not every spirit, but try the spirits whether they are of God: because many false prophets are gone out into the world" (1John 4:1).

We must not believe every teacher who professes to have a divine commission to preach but test such, whether they be of God; and the more so because many false prophets are gone out into the world.

We can distinguish those who embrace the truth from those who do not. The Bible advises us not to believe every teacher who professes to have a divine commission to preach, but test such, whether they are of God because many false prophets are gone out into the world. Thus, before you partner with any pastor, test the spirit and make sure the spirit that animates in this person is the Spirit of God. If the Spirit of God is in Him, God will reveal. The evidence of true piety is to perceive from God.

"He that is of God heareth God's words: ye, therefore, hear them not, because ye are not of God" (John 8:47).

"We are of God: he that knoweth God heareth us; he that is not of God heareth not us. Hereby know we the spirit of truth, and the spirit of error" (1Jo 4:6).

Chapter Four

The Manipulation

According to Dictionary.com, manipulation is "to juggle; to falsify; to manage or influence skillfully, especially in an unfair manner" Many of these asserted pastors are skillfully fraudulent. They destroyed people's souls by the poison of their doctrine. The diseased they claimed they have strengthened, they did not; the sick and the brokenhearted they claimed they have healed, were lies to attract attention and importance to themselves in the eyes of people. With force and cruelty, they manipulate, rule and deceive people. They put people in perpetual bondage and spiritual slavery and device all kinds of falsehood to sustain their godless empires.

Using God's Name in Vain

Doesn't it grieve you brethren, that the name of our God is being taken in vain and desecrated? Doesn't it grieve you that we are living in such a godless age and time that people don't care about how God feels? In today's world, it is with no dispute a taboo to defile or desecrate the name of Satan, but when it pertains to the name of the Almighty God, people tend to use it without fear and reverence.

Regardless of what you think, it is inexcusable to use the name of the Almighty God in vain. God will not hold us guiltless. He will account us guilty and punish us for it.

> *"Thou shalt not take the name of the LORD thy God in vain; for the LORD will not hold him guiltless that taketh his name in vain" (Ex 20:7).*

> *Using God's name in profanity is perhaps the simplest, most effective way these false men of God show their contempt toward our Creator. Godly Jews won't even speak God's name because it is so holy, yet unrepentant man uses it to express a strong feeling of repugnance. "Mine heart within me is broken because of the prophets; all my bones shake; I am like a drunken man, and like a man whom wine hath overcome, because of the LORD, and because of the words of his holiness. For both prophet and priest are profane; yea, in my house, have I found their wickedness, saith the LORD" (Jer. 23:9, 11).*

Jeremiah was a man with empathy, who was troubled because of the false doctrine the prophets preached in his days and the wicked lives they lived. His heart was oppressed with grief and vexation to hear these false prophets making use of God's name in vain, and pretended to have heard from Him.

Today, we see the rising number of voices claiming to speak for God around the world. They are all over the world manipulating and using God's name in vain. They practice heresies; they are psychopaths. They have no remorse of the harm they inflict on people. The indecency and obscenity they bring to the Body of Christ are without measure. Everyone who follows them will be compelled to suffer the bitterest part of the Lord's indignation.

Some Traits Of A Psychopath

- Pathological Lying
- Need For Stimulation
- Grandiose Sense Of Self
- Lack Of Remorse Or Guilt
- Cunning And Manipulative
- Glib And Superficial Charm
- Shallow Emotional Response
- Callousness And Lack Of Empathy

The list continues. Watch out for these traits in these deceitful men and women.

"Let no man deceive you with vain words: for because of these things cometh the wrath of God upon the children of disobedience" (Ephesians 5:6).

Today many preachers are deceiving many with empty words; some say there's no hell, no wrath, God condones the human behavior, but they are deceiving themselves and gullible people. Surely, the wrath of God will be fiercer on those who teach such lies and neglect the message of holiness and salvation from the pulpit and in their lifestyle.

Never has the Lord and the words of His holiness so abused and distorted by these so-called pastors. The dishonor done to God's holy name, and the desecration of His holy word is the greatest grief imaginable. They dishonor the name of God by rash and false swearing. They thought they have a great deal of resolution when people praise them. People that run after them don't know that their heart is fully set to do evil. They are not valiant for the truth and have no courage to break off their evil courses. They are slaves of sin.

"He also will drink the wine of God's wrath, poured full strength into the cup of his anger, and he will be tormented with fire and sulfur in the presence of the holy angels and

in the presence of the Lamb. And the smoke of their torment goes up forever and ever, and they have no rest, day or night, these worshipers of the beast and its image, and whoever receives the mark of its name" (Revelation 14:10-11).

God's wrath is just, and as real as His mercy, love, and forgiveness, but the forgiveness of God has been placed on His Son for all who have repented and then trusted in Christ. Those that trust in their good works will drink from the cup of the wrath of God. Sadly, most people will.

The days of God's wrath is coming just as surely as the sun rises tomorrow morning, and when that day comes, it will be too late to ask for mercy, for each man and woman will be judged according to their works. No doubt, there will be some of us that will read this and reject it, but on that day, you will never forget this warning. I pray this will not be your experience in that day of divine reckoning.

Ordinances of God Profaned

These false men of God continue to profane the ordinances of God as they pretend to administer. All their conversation are profane, and it is not strange that the people they lead are so perverted. God found these false pastors to be wicked and guilty, both of idolatry and immorality. They teach people to sin by their examples. They cause many people to err, and to forsake the service of the true God and worship idol. It is the same spirit of error that perverted the priesthood in the Old Testament.

> *"Ye shall make you no idols nor graven image, neither rear you up a standing image, neither shall ye set up any image of stone in your land, to bow down unto it: for I am the LORD your God" (Lev 26:1).*

Idolatry is perhaps the greatest of all sins because it opens the door to unrestrained evil. It gives sinners license not only to tolerate sin but also to sanction it. When one makes gods he is comfortable with, in his own image, he creates his own moral standards to go along with it.

God is the fountain of power, and no intelligent creature can be empowered but through him. Therefore, whoever seeks power in the creature is, in reality, an idolater, who puts the creature in the place of the Creator. Expecting that from the gratification of his passions, he is a good servant of God.

We are to have no other gods before the one true God. He is to be preeminent in our hearts. We are required to love God above all other beings or things, and with all the faculties of our minds. Jesus said:

> *"The first of all the commandments is, Hear, O Israel; The Lord, our God, is one Lord: And thou shalt love the*

Lord thy God with all thy heart, and with all thy soul, and with all thy mind, and with all thy strength: this is the first commandment" (Mark 12:29-30).

Lies in God's Name

It is horrible that false pastors use the name of the holy God, and yet they walk in lies and wallow in darkness and all manner of impurity. The words that come out of their mouths are all either jest and banter, fraud and design. They target and prophesy to those who are desperately in need that walks after the imagination of their own hearts. They caress and flatter themselves to be seen as true servants of God. They hypnotize people, and with daring words of what God has not said, those desperate are resolved to believe their strong delusions. They are anointed by Satan to mesmerize their audience with lying spirit.

"Thus saith the LORD of hosts, Hearken not unto the words of the prophets that prophesy unto you: they make you vain: they speak a vision of their own heart, and not out of the mouth of the LORD" (Jer. 23:16).

"The prophets prophesy lies in my name: I sent them not, neither have I commanded them, neither spake unto them: they prophesy unto you a false vision and divination, and a thing of naught, and the deceit of their heart" (Jer. 14:14).

God has not sent these pastors; they never had any mission from God. He never chose them in any service of His Kingdom. They represent the kingdom of darkness, and with the aids of their assistance, they use delusional device and a crafty scheme to trick people and call it the power of God.

> *"How long will this be in the heart of the prophets who prophesy lies? Indeed they are prophets of the deceit of their own heart, "who try to make My people forget My name by their dreams which everyone tells his neighbor, as their fathers forgot My name for Baal....What is the chaff to the wheat?" says the LORD. "Is not My word like a fire?" says the LORD, "And like a hammer that breaks the rock in pieces? "Therefore behold, I am against the prophets," says the LORD, "who steal My words everyone from his neighbor. "Behold, I am against the prophets," says the LORD, "who use their tongues and say, 'He says.' "Behold, I am against those who prophesy false dreams," says the LORD, "and tell them, and cause My people to err by their lies and by their recklessness. Yet I did not send them or command them; therefore they shall not profit this person at all," says the LORD....'And I will bring an everlasting reproach upon you, and a perpetual shame, which shall not be forgotten." (Jeremiah 23:26-31, 40).*

God gave this warning to everyone. This punishment which He threatened shall surely take place; a short time will determine it. If you are one of the partners of these false pastors, repent and remain faithful, or you shall not escape the wrath.

The Influence of God

"For "who has known the mind of the LORD that he may instruct Him?" But we have the mind of Christ" (1 Corinthians 2:16).

The Apostle Paul's argument here is this: "No one can understand God. No one can fully comprehend His plans, feelings, views, and His designs. No one by nature, under the influence of sense and passion, is either disposed to investigate His truths when they are revealed. But the servants of God are influenced by God. With His influence, we have His Spirit and can comprehend His feelings, desires, purposes, and plans.

These false pastors have no Spirit of God and cannot perceive or hear from Him. They do not speak about Him, nor stand in His counsels. Their confidence and consultation are not of the Lord. Though they try to deliver their messages with a great deal of assurance. If they had stood in God's counsel, as they pretend, they would have made the scriptures and His commandments their standard.

Reflection

Personal Notes:_____

_____

_____

_____

_____

_____

_____

_____

Guided Action Plan

_____

_____

_____

_____

_____

_____

Chapter Five

God Is Aware

*"I have heard what the prophets have said who prophesy
lies in My name, saying, 'I have dreamed, I have dreamed!'
"How long will this be in the heart of the prophets who
prophesy lies? Indeed, they are prophets of the deceit of
their own heart" (Jeremiah 23:25-26).*

Pastors who are engaged with false teaching thought
God is so attentively engaged with the myriads of
events happening in the universe that He had no
leisure or time to take cognizance of what they are doing.
They forget that God is omniscience; that He knows that
they speak visions of their own hearts; that they tell lies,
and have the effrontery to make God the patron of their

lies and made-up stories. They forgot that God knows that all of them are involved in the worship of false gods, and their teachings encourage and influence people to sin. God knows that their works are not for Him and they are raising souls for the devil.

They forgot God knows all their impostures, and all the spurious imitation they have put in the world. When they manipulate and tell people, they have heard from God when they have not, God knows. All the methods they use to deceive people; the abuse and counterfeit revelation they give people, God sees them all. They frequently mention the name of Jesus and prefaced all they said with, "Thus saith the Lord," God hears.

> "Is not My word like a fire?" says the LORD, "And like a hammer that breaks the rock in pieces?" (Jer. 23:29).

> "Because you speak this word, Behold, I will make My words in your mouth fire, And this people wood, And it shall devour them" (Jer. 5:12-14).

Divine Judgments

How can anyone be safe, or at ease, that have the Almighty power of God against him? All the pastors brainwashing and deluding people, God is proclaiming wrath against them. They stand indicted, for robbery, killing and destroying lives.

It is of great significance to know that these people that come to you in God's name make more mischief to the power of godliness than false prophets who practice voodoo. God's anger is on them and shall not return, for the decree has gone forth. God will not alter his mind, nor suffer His anger to be turned away until He has executed the sentence and perform the thoughts of His heart. God's "Woe!" is also out of compassion for the victims of these self-serving pastors.

"But the fearful, and unbelieving, and the abominable, and murderers, and whoremongers, and sorcerers, and idolaters, and all liars, shall have their part in the lake which burneth with fire and brimstone: which is the second death."(Revelation 21:8).

"Thus I will punish the world for its evil and the wicked for their iniquity; I will also put an end to the arrogance of the proud and abase the haughtiness of the ruthless" (Isaiah 13:11).

God's wrath comes with decisive and fierce judgement and should not be taken for granted. It is to be reckoned those perverting the words of God for their personal interest are wicked."

God promised to punish those perverting His words; whether they are pastors or regular church members.

Their compromise will bring severe judgments and curses upon their families. Every person's sins shall be on his own head. The guilt of these sins shall be so heavy upon them as to sink them into the pit of hell.

> *"Therefore thus saith the LORD God of Israel against the pastors that feed my people; Ye have scattered my flock, and driven them away, and have not visited them: behold, I will visit upon you the evil of your doings, saith the LORD"* (Jeremiah 23:2).

Divine judgment is presented as a necessary response to an intolerable situation. Those who run after these false pastors, your punishments also awaits you, because you failed to test the spirit. If you are among followers of these fake pastors, you are advised to retract your errors and repent.

The impenitent heart is like a rock. If it is not melted by the word of God as the fire, then it will be broken to pieces by the sledge hammer of God's word. Whatever opposition that confronts and resists the word of God, shall be borne down and broken to pieces. You must consider the punishment while you continue in this course God hates.

> *"Therefore, behold, I am against the prophets, saith the LORD, that steal my words everyone from his neighbour.*

Behold, I am against the prophets, saith the LORD, that use their tongues, and say, He saith. Behold, I am against them that prophesy false dreams, saith the LORD, and do tell them, and cause my people to err by their lies, and by their lightness; yet I sent them not, nor commanded them: therefore they shall not profit this people at all, saith the LORD" (Jeremiah 23:30-32).

Reflection

Personal Notes: _____

_____

_____

_____

_____

_____

_____

_____

Guided Action Plan

_____

_____

_____

_____

_____

_____

Chapter Six

It Is Your Fault

Desperation leads to destruction. If you are deceived and misled by these false pastors, the fault is yours. You have no one to blame. You will suffer the wrath of God. On that day your excuses cannot redeem you. Deception will be rife in the Last Days we are living in now. Jesus warned us about it and puts the responsibility of not being deceived on us. This happened when His disciples asked Him about the Last Days and His return to earth.

> "And as he sat upon the mount of Olives, the disciples came unto him privately, saying, Tell us, when shall these things be? And what shall be the sign of thy coming, and of the end of the world? And Jesus answered and said unto

them, Take heed that no man deceive you. For many shall come in my name, saying, I am Christ; and shall deceive many" (Matthew 24:3-5).

The Lord is God of mercy, but not on the judgment day. Repent now that you still have time. Leave any church whose ways of serving God is questionable and inconsistent with the Bible. Ignorant is not an excuse before the Lord. By prayer, test everyone's spirit. May the Lord grant you discernment.

> *"Beloved, believe not every spirit, but try the spirits whether they are of God: because many false prophets are gone out into the world" (1John 4:1).*

Do not confide implicitly in everyone who professes to be under the influences of the Holy Spirit. You must not believe everyone who professes to have a divine commission to preach, but try such, whether they are of God. Do not be forward to believe everyone who claims to be a man sent by God. The true and the false pastors alike are claiming to be under the influence of the Spirit of God, and it is of a great significance that all such pretensions be examined by the light of His word and the Spirit. Put the persons under the divine radar and measure them by the standards of the Bible. Check and test what spirit influences them. Try them by that testimony emanating from the Spirit of God.

You are not obligated to admit everyone who claimed to have been sent from God. The fact that they claim they are sent does not authenticate their claim. Such claim must be subjected to proper proof before it is conceded to. All pretensions to divine inspiration are to be examined by the proper tests because many delusive pastors in the world set up such claims.

Before they skillfully influence you with flattering words, check the fruits of their doctrines in their lives. If their lives correspond with God's commandments, receive them as true servants of God. If not, you are to reject them and hold them to be impostors.

> "If any man teach otherwise, and consent not to wholesome words, even the words of our Lord Jesus Christ, and to the doctrine which is according to godliness; He is proud, knowing nothing, but doting about questions and strifes of words, whereof cometh envy, strife, railings, evil surmisings, Perverse disputings of men of corrupt minds, and destitute of the truth, supposing that gain is godliness: from such withdraw thyself" (1 Timothy 6:3-5).

Be wise, and avoid these false men and women of God that practice heresy. Give them no access and have no fellowship with them. Try to distinguish those who embrace the truth from those who do not. Whatever pretensions they might set up for piety, it is clear that if they did not embrace the doctrines taught by the Lord, they could not be regarded as God's servants, or as true Christians.

Satan's Scheme

It has been the artifice of Satan, in all ages, to obstruct the efficacy of sacred things by turning them into the hands of false ministers of the gospel. If you look upon God as you ought to do in His greatness and goodness and be duly sensible of your relationship and obligation to Him, you will not be a victim by any false pastor.

> *"If any of you lack wisdom, let him ask of God, that giveth to all men liberally, and upbraideth not; and it shall be given him. But let him ask in faith, nothing wavering. For he that wavereth is like a wave of the sea driven with the wind and tossed" (Jas 1:5).*

It is a commendable practice to enquire after the mind of God and to enquire of these pastors what they say and do, and what they claimed they heard from God before partnering with them. This we must do with a right mind.

> *"When I say to the wicked, 'You will surely die,' and you do not warn him or speak out to warn the wicked from his wicked way that he may live, that wicked man shall die in his iniquity, but his blood I will require at your hand" (Ezekiel 3:18).*

Note, the word of the Lord can never fail. God's word will be magnified and made honorable when those that mock at it shall be vilified and made contemptible.

> *"Verily I say unto you, this generation shall not pass, till all these things be fulfilled"* (Mt 24:34).

Indeed, it will be miserable that you are forsaken and forgotten about God.

Reflection

Personal Notes:_____

_____

_____

_____

_____

_____

_____

_____

_____

Guided Action Plan

_____

_____

_____

_____

_____

_____

Chapter Seven

Be Warned!

"But with whom was he grieved forty years? was it not with them that had sinned, whose carcasses fell in the wilderness?" (Hebrews 3:17).

Our continual enjoyment of the favor of God's is dependent on our faithfulness to His grace. If we rebel, though God had chosen us through His love in Christ Jesus, yet He will cast us off in His justice. A distinct example is the 24,000 whose carcasses fell in the wilderness because they had sinned; yet these were of the elect that came out of Egypt (Number 14:29). The elect, we see, may become unfaithful, and reprobate. Therefore, take heed to your salvation and remain steadfast till the end.

"Incline your ear, and come to Me. Hear, and your soul shall live; And I will make an everlasting covenant with you" (1 Isa 55:3).

Nothing effectually corrupts and perverts a nation like debauchery of false pastors and prophets. Those that follow them are warned. If you give deaf ears, you shall have no comfort in your way. God had warned us not to give any credit to these fake pastors; for, though they flattered you with hopes of impunity, the judgments of God would certainly break out against anyone who follows them, unless you repented.

Take Notice Of What God Says

"You shall make no covenant with them, nor with their gods" (Exodus 23:32).

Listen not to the words of these false pastors. God's word shall stand firm, and not yours or theirs. God's word will build you up, but theirs will make you vain and famished. They feed you with vain hopes, which will fail you at last. They tell you, no evil shall come upon you, but hear what God says in His wrath:

"Behold, a whirlwind of the LORD has gone forth in a fury-A violent whirlwind! It will fall violently on the head of the wicked." (Jeremiah 23: 19).

They tell you, all shall be calmed and unruffled, but God tells you, there is a storm coming; a whirlwind of the Lord spinning, and there is no standing before it. It is a whirlwind raised by divine wrath, and it has gone forth in a fury. A wind that is brought forth out of the treasuries of divine vengeance; thus it is a grievous whirlwind, and shall come heavily with rain and hail, upon the head of these wicked pastors who deceived the people. They cannot avoid it nor find any shelter unless they repent and mend their ways. Our God is merciful and just.

"Upon the wicked, he shall rain snares, fire and brimstone, and a horrible tempest: this shall be the portion of their cup" (Psalm. 11:6).

This sentence is bound and is irreversible and irrevocable. The anger of the Lord shall not return; the decree has gone forth. God will not alter his mind, nor suffer His anger to be turned away until He has executed the sentence and performed the thoughts of His heart. God's whirlwind, when it comes down from heaven, shall not return back to Him.

"But it shall accomplish what I please, and it shall prosper in the thing for which I sent It" (Isa. 55:11).

As a perfect example, here is the story of Sodom and Gomorrah, written for our learning.

"And there came two angels to Sodom at even; and Lot sat in the gate of Sodom: and Lot seeing them rose up to

meet them; and he bowed himself with his face toward the ground; And he said, Behold now, my lords, turn in, I pray you, into your servant's house, and tarry all night, and wash your feet, and ye shall rise up early, and go on your ways. And they said, nay; but we will abide in the street all night. And he pressed upon them greatly, and they turned in unto him and entered into his house, and he made them a feast and did bake unleavened bread, and they did eat. But before they lay down, the men of the city, even the men of Sodom, compassed the house round, both old and young, all the people from every quarter: And they called unto Lot, and said unto him, where are the men which came into thee this night? Bring them out unto us, that we may know them. And Lot went out at the door unto them, and shut the door after him, And said, I pray you, brethren, do not so wickedly. Behold now, I have two daughters which have not known man; let me, I pray you, bring them out unto you, and do ye to them as is good in your eyes: only unto these men do nothing; for therefore came they under the shadow of my roof. And they said, Stand back. And they said again, this one fellow came into sojourn, and he will needs be a judge: now will we deal worse with thee, than with them. And they pressed sore upon the man, even Lot, and came near to break the door. But the men put forth their hand, and pulled Lot into the house to them, and shut to the door. And they smote the men that were at the door of the house with blindness, *both small and great: so that they wearied themselves to find the door. And the men said unto Lot, Hast thou here any besides? Son in law, and thy sons, and thy daughters, and whatsoever thou hast in the city, bring them out of this place: For we will destroy this place because the cry of them is waxen great before the face of the LORD; and the LORD hath sent us to destroy it. Then the LORD rained upon Sodom and upon "Gomorrah brimstone and fire from the LORD out of heaven; and he overthrew those cities, and all the plain, and all the inhabitants of the cities, and that which grew upon the ground" (Gen. 19:1-13, 24-25).*

These false pastors will not consider this now, but in the latter days, they shall consider it perfectly. What a fearful thing to fall into the hands of a just and jealous God? Those that will not consider it now will want to when it is too late.

" It is a fearful thing to fall into the hands of the living God" (Hebrews 10:31).

"For our God is a consuming fire" (Hebrews 12:29).

Proverbs Advised:

"Hear, my children, the instruction of a father, and give attention to know to understand; for I give you good doctrine: Do not forsake my law" (Pr. 4:1-2)

"And he said unto them, He that hath ears to hear let him hear" (Mark. 4:9).